A Gratitude Journal *for*

NATURE LOVERS

A 52 WEEK JOURNAL
WITH GRATITUDE PROMPTS

SUSAN PATON

ISBN: 1536853224
ISBN-13: 978-1536853223

This journal belongs to

_____

Year _____

I am grateful for...

I am grateful for
this beginning...

This week, I am particularly grateful for:

_____

_____

_____

_____

_____

I am grateful for...

Monday
_____

_____

_____

Tuesday
_____

_____

_____

Wednesday
_____

_____

_____

Thursday
_____

_____

_____

Friday
_____

_____

_____

Saturday
_____

_____

_____

Sunday
_____

_____

_____

I am grateful for...

I am grateful for
this part of winter...

This week, I am particularly grateful for:

_____

_____

_____

_____

_____

I am grateful for...

Monday
_____

_____

_____

Tuesday
_____

_____

_____

Wednesday
_____

_____

_____

Thursday
_____

_____

_____

Friday
_____

_____

_____

Saturday
_____

_____

_____

Sunday
_____

_____

_____

I am grateful for...

*I am grateful
for this place...*

This week I am particularly grateful for:

[handwritten letter practice: Y, Yb, Yb, Bb, YByb, YByb, Bbyyb, etc.]

I am grateful for...

Monday
_____

_____

_____

Tuesday
_____

_____

_____

Wednesday
_____

_____

_____

Thursday
_____

_____

_____

Friday
_____

_____

_____

Saturday
_____

_____

_____

Sunday
_____

_____

_____

I am grateful for...

I am grateful for this memory...

This week I am particularly grateful for:

_____

_____

_____

_____

_____

I am grateful for...

Monday

_____

_____

_____

Tuesday

_____

_____

_____

Wednesday

_____

_____

_____

Thursday

_____

_____

_____

Friday

_____

_____

_____

Saturday

_____

_____

_____

Sunday

_____

_____

_____

I am grateful for...

I am
grateful for
this gift...

This week I am particularly grateful for:

_____

_____

_____

_____

_____

I am grateful for...

Monday _____

_____

_____

Tuesday _____

_____

_____

Wednesday _____

_____

_____

Thursday _____

_____

_____

Friday _____

_____

_____

Saturday _____

_____

_____

Sunday _____

_____

_____

I am grateful for...

I am grateful for this vacation...

This week I am particularly grateful for:

_____

_____

_____

_____

_____

I am grateful for...

Monday
_____

_____

_____

Tuesday
_____

_____

_____

Wednesday
_____

_____

_____

Thursday
_____

_____

_____

Friday
_____

_____

_____

Saturday
_____

_____

_____

Sunday
_____

_____

_____

I am grateful for...

I am grateful
for this challenge...

This week I am particularly grateful for:

_____

_____

_____

_____

_____

I am grateful for...

Monday _____

_____

_____

Tuesday _____

_____

_____

Wednesday _____

_____

_____

Thursday _____

_____

_____

Friday _____

_____

_____

Saturday _____

_____

_____

Sunday _____

_____

_____

I am grateful for...

I am grateful for
this sound...

This week I am particularly grateful for:

_____

_____

_____

_____

_____

I am grateful for...

Monday

_____

_____

_____

Tuesday

_____

_____

_____

Wednesday

_____

_____

_____

Thursday

_____

_____

_____

Friday

_____

_____

_____

Saturday

_____

_____

_____

Sunday

_____

_____

_____

I am grateful for...

I am grateful for

this season...

This week, I am particularly grateful for:

_____

_____

_____

_____

_____

I am grateful for...

Monday
_____

_____

_____

Tuesday
_____

_____

_____

Wednesday
_____

_____

_____

Thursday
_____

_____

_____

Friday
_____

_____

_____

Saturday
_____

_____

_____

Sunday
_____

_____

_____

I am grateful for...

I am grateful
for this value...

This week I am particularly grateful for:

_____

_____

_____

_____

_____

I am grateful for...

Monday
_____

_____

_____

Tuesday
_____

_____

_____

Wednesday
_____

_____

_____

Thursday
_____

_____

_____

Friday
_____

_____

_____

Saturday
_____

_____

_____

Sunday
_____

_____

_____

I am grateful for...

I am grateful
for this chance...

This week I am particularly grateful for:

_____

_____

_____

_____

_____

I am grateful for...

Monday

_____

_____

_____

Tuesday

_____

_____

_____

Wednesday

_____

_____

_____

Thursday

_____

_____

_____

Friday

_____

_____

_____

Saturday

_____

_____

_____

Sunday

_____

_____

_____

I am grateful for...

I am grateful
for this perseverance...

This week, I am particularly grateful for:

_____

_____

_____

_____

_____

I am grateful for...

Monday
_____

_____

_____

Tuesday
_____

_____

_____

Wednesday
_____

_____

_____

Thursday
_____

_____

_____

Friday
_____

_____

_____

Saturday
_____

_____

_____

Sunday
_____

_____

_____

I am grateful for...

I am grateful for
this color...

This week I am particularly grateful for:

_____

_____

_____

_____

_____

I am grateful for...

Monday

_____

_____

_____

Tuesday

_____

_____

_____

Wednesday

_____

_____

_____

Thursday

_____

_____

_____

Friday

_____

_____

_____

Saturday

_____

_____

_____

Sunday

_____

_____

_____

I am grateful for...

I am grateful for
this sign of spring...

This week, I am particularly grateful for:

_____

_____

_____

_____

_____

I am grateful for...

Monday _____

_____

_____

Tuesday _____

_____

_____

Wednesday _____

_____

_____

Thursday _____

_____

_____

Friday _____

_____

_____

Saturday _____

_____

_____

Sunday _____

_____

_____

I am grateful for...

I am grateful for

this journey...

This week I am particularly grateful for:

_____

_____

_____

_____

_____

I am grateful for...

Monday

_____

_____

_____

Tuesday

_____

_____

_____

Wednesday

_____

_____

_____

Thursday

_____

_____

_____

Friday

_____

_____

_____

Saturday

_____

_____

_____

Sunday

_____

_____

_____

I am grateful for...

I am grateful
for this insight...

This week I am particularly grateful for:

_____

_____

_____

_____

_____

I am grateful for...

Monday

_____

_____

_____

Tuesday

_____

_____

_____

Wednesday

_____

_____

_____

Thursday

_____

_____

_____

Friday

_____

_____

_____

Saturday

_____

_____

_____

Sunday

_____

_____

_____

I am grateful for...

I am grateful for
this change...

This week I am particularly grateful for:

_____

_____

_____

_____

_____

I am grateful for...

Monday
_____

_____

_____

Tuesday
_____

_____

_____

Wednesday
_____

_____

_____

Thursday
_____

_____

_____

Friday
_____

_____

_____

Saturday
_____

_____

_____

Sunday
_____

_____

_____

I am grateful for...

I am grateful for this task...

This week I am particularly grateful for:

_____

_____

_____

_____

_____

I am grateful for...

Monday
_____
_____
_____

Tuesday
_____
_____
_____

Wednesday
_____
_____
_____

Thursday
_____
_____
_____

Friday
_____
_____
_____

Saturday
_____
_____
_____

Sunday
_____
_____
_____

I am grateful for...

I am grateful for

these imperfections...

This week I am particularly grateful for:

_____

_____

_____

_____

_____

I am grateful for...

Monday

_____

_____

_____

Tuesday

_____

_____

_____

Wednesday

_____

_____

_____

Thursday

_____

_____

_____

Friday

_____

_____

_____

Saturday

_____

_____

_____

Sunday

_____

_____

_____

I am grateful for...

I am grateful for this strength...

This week I am particularly grateful for:

_____

_____

_____

_____

_____

I am grateful for...

Monday
_____

_____

Tuesday
_____

_____

Wednesday
_____

_____

Thursday
_____

_____

Friday
_____

_____

Saturday
_____

_____

Sunday
_____

_____

I am grateful for...

I am grateful
for this pattern...

This week I am particularly grateful for:

_____

_____

_____

_____

_____

I am grateful for...

Monday

_____

_____

Tuesday

_____

_____

Wednesday

_____

_____

Thursday

_____

_____

Friday

_____

_____

Saturday

_____

_____

Sunday

_____

_____

I am grateful for...

I am grateful for
this opportunity to grow...

This week I am particularly grateful for:

_____

_____

_____

_____

_____

I am grateful for...

Monday
_____
_____
_____

Tuesday
_____
_____
_____

Wednesday
_____
_____
_____

Thursday
_____
_____
_____

Friday
_____
_____
_____

Saturday
_____
_____
_____

Sunday
_____
_____
_____

I am grateful for...

I am grateful for
this history...

This week I am particularly grateful for:

_____

_____

_____

_____

_____

I am grateful for...

Monday

_____

_____

_____

Tuesday

_____

_____

_____

Wednesday

_____

_____

_____

Thursday

_____

_____

_____

Friday

_____

_____

_____

Saturday

_____

_____

_____

Sunday

_____

_____

_____

I am grateful for...

I am grateful for
this relationship...

This week I am particularly grateful for:

_____

_____

_____

_____

_____

I am grateful for...

Monday
_____

_____

_____

Tuesday
_____

_____

_____

Wednesday
_____

_____

_____

Thursday
_____

_____

_____

Friday
_____

_____

_____

Saturday
_____

_____

_____

Sunday
_____

_____

_____

I am grateful for...

I am grateful for
this obstacle...

This week I am particularly grateful for:

_____

_____

_____

_____

_____

I am grateful for...

Monday
_____

_____

_____

Tuesday
_____

_____

_____

Wednesday
_____

_____

_____

Thursday
_____

_____

_____

Friday
_____

_____

_____

Saturday
_____

_____

_____

Sunday
_____

_____

_____

I am grateful for...

I am grateful for this disorder...

This week, I am particularly grateful for:

_____

_____

_____

_____

_____

I am grateful for...

Monday
_____

_____

_____

Tuesday
_____

_____

_____

Wednesday
_____

_____

_____

Thursday
_____

_____

_____

Friday
_____

_____

_____

Saturday
_____

_____

_____

Sunday
_____

_____

_____

I am grateful for...

*I am grateful for
this part of summer...*

This week I am particularly grateful for:

_____

_____

_____

_____

_____

I am grateful for...

Monday

_____

_____

_____

Tuesday

_____

_____

_____

Wednesday

_____

_____

_____

Thursday

_____

_____

_____

Friday

_____

_____

_____

Saturday

_____

_____

_____

Sunday

_____

_____

_____

I am grateful for...

I am grateful for
this choice...

This week I am particularly grateful for:

_____

_____

_____

_____

_____

I am grateful for...

Monday
_____

_____

_____

Tuesday
_____

_____

_____

Wednesday
_____

_____

_____

Thursday
_____

_____

_____

Friday
_____

_____

_____

Saturday
_____

_____

_____

Sunday
_____

_____

_____

I am grateful for...

I am grateful for
this lesson...

This week I am particularly grateful for:

_____

_____

_____

_____

_____

I am grateful for...

Monday
_____

_____

_____

Tuesday
_____

_____

_____

Wednesday
_____

_____

_____

Thursday
_____

_____

_____

Friday
_____

_____

_____

Saturday
_____

_____

_____

Sunday
_____

_____

_____

I am grateful for...

I am grateful for
this vitality...

This week I am particularly grateful for:

_____

_____

_____

_____

_____

I am grateful for...

Monday _____

_____

Tuesday _____

_____

Wednesday _____

_____

Thursday _____

_____

Friday _____

_____

Saturday _____

_____

Sunday _____

_____

_____

I am grateful for...

I am grateful for this whimsy...

This week I am particularly grateful for:

_____

_____

_____

_____

_____

I am grateful for...

Monday
_____

_____

_____

Tuesday
_____

_____

_____

Wednesday
_____

_____

_____

Thursday
_____

_____

_____

Friday
_____

_____

_____

Saturday
_____

_____

_____

Sunday
_____

_____

_____

I am grateful for...

I am grateful
for this adventure...

This week I am particularly grateful for:

_____

_____

_____

_____

_____

I am grateful for...

Monday

_____

_____

_____

Tuesday

_____

_____

_____

Wednesday

_____

_____

_____

Thursday

_____

_____

_____

Friday

_____

_____

_____

Saturday

_____

_____

_____

Sunday

_____

_____

_____

I am grateful for...

I am grateful for
this tradition...

This week I am particularly grateful for:

_____

_____

_____

_____

_____

I am grateful for...

Monday

_____

_____

_____

Tuesday

_____

_____

_____

Wednesday

_____

_____

_____

Thursday

_____

_____

_____

Friday

_____

_____

_____

Saturday

_____

_____

_____

Sunday

_____

_____

_____

I am grateful for...

I am grateful for
this reflection...

This week I am particularly grateful for:

_____

_____

_____

_____

_____

I am grateful for...

Monday
_____
_____
_____

Tuesday
_____
_____
_____

Wednesday
_____
_____
_____

Thursday
_____
_____
_____

Friday
_____
_____
_____

Saturday
_____
_____
_____

Sunday
_____
_____
_____

I am grateful for...

I am grateful for

this new direction...

This week I am particularly grateful for:

_____

_____

_____

_____

_____

I am grateful for...

Monday _____

_____

Tuesday _____

_____

Wednesday _____

_____

Thursday _____

_____

Friday _____

_____

Saturday _____

_____

Sunday _____

_____

_____

I am grateful for...

I am grateful for

these roots...

This week I am particularly grateful for:

_____

_____

_____

_____

_____

I am grateful for...

Monday
_____

_____

_____

Tuesday
_____

_____

_____

Wednesday
_____

_____

_____

Thursday
_____

_____

_____

Friday
_____

_____

_____

Saturday
_____

_____

_____

Sunday
_____

_____

_____

I am grateful for...

I am grateful
for this emotion...

This week I am particularly grateful for:

_____

_____

_____

_____

_____

I am grateful for...

Monday
_____

_____

_____

Tuesday
_____

_____

_____

Wednesday
_____

_____

_____

Thursday
_____

_____

_____

Friday
_____

_____

_____

Saturday
_____

_____

_____

Sunday
_____

_____

_____

I am grateful for...

I am grateful
for this age...

This week I am particularly grateful for:

_____

_____

_____

_____

_____

I am grateful for...

Monday
_____

_____

_____

Tuesday
_____

_____

_____

Wednesday
_____

_____

_____

Thursday
_____

_____

_____

Friday
_____

_____

_____

Saturday
_____

_____

_____

Sunday
_____

_____

_____

I am grateful for...

I am grateful for this truth...

This week I am particularly grateful for:

_____

_____

_____

_____

_____

I am grateful for...

Monday
_____

_____

_____

Tuesday
_____

_____

_____

Wednesday
_____

_____

_____

Thursday
_____

_____

_____

Friday
_____

_____

_____

Saturday
_____

_____

_____

Sunday
_____

_____

_____

I am grateful for...

I am grateful for
this part of autumn...

This week I am particularly grateful for:

_____

_____

_____

_____

_____

I am grateful for...

Monday
_____
_____
_____

Tuesday
_____
_____
_____

Wednesday
_____
_____
_____

Thursday
_____
_____
_____

Friday
_____
_____
_____

Saturday
_____
_____
_____

Sunday
_____
_____
_____

I am grateful for...

I am grateful for
this freedom...

This week I am particularly grateful for:

_____

_____

_____

_____

_____

I am grateful for...

Monday
_____

_____

_____

Tuesday
_____

_____

_____

Wednesday
_____

_____

_____

Thursday
_____

_____

_____

Friday
_____

_____

_____

Saturday
_____

_____

_____

Sunday
_____

_____

_____

I am grateful for...

I am grateful for this support...

This week I am particularly grateful for:

_____

_____

_____

_____

_____

I am grateful for...

Monday _____

_____

_____

Tuesday _____

_____

_____

Wednesday _____

_____

_____

Thursday _____

_____

_____

Friday _____

_____

_____

Saturday _____

_____

_____

Sunday _____

_____

_____

I am grateful for...

I am grateful for
this simple pleasure...

This week I am particularly grateful for:

_____

_____

_____

_____

_____

I am grateful for...

Monday

_____

_____

_____

Tuesday

_____

_____

_____

Wednesday

_____

_____

_____

Thursday

_____

_____

_____

Friday

_____

_____

_____

Saturday

_____

_____

_____

Sunday

_____

_____

_____

I am grateful for...

I am grateful
for this hope...

This week I am particularly grateful for:

_____

_____

_____

_____

_____

I am grateful for...

Monday
_____

_____

_____

Tuesday
_____

_____

_____

Wednesday
_____

_____

_____

Thursday
_____

_____

_____

Friday
_____

_____

_____

Saturday
_____

_____

_____

Sunday
_____

_____

_____

I am grateful for...

I am grateful
for this idea...

This week I am particularly grateful for:

_____

_____

_____

_____

_____

I am grateful for...

Monday
_____

_____

_____

Tuesday
_____

_____

_____

Wednesday
_____

_____

_____

Thursday
_____

_____

_____

Friday
_____

_____

_____

Saturday
_____

_____

_____

Sunday
_____

_____

_____

I am grateful for...

I am grateful for this beauty...

This week I am particularly grateful for:

_____

_____

_____

_____

_____

I am grateful for...

Monday
_____

_____

_____

Tuesday
_____

_____

_____

Wednesday
_____

_____

_____

Thursday
_____

_____

_____

Friday
_____

_____

_____

Saturday
_____

_____

_____

Sunday
_____

_____

_____

I am grateful for...

I am grateful for
this fragility...

This week I am particularly grateful for:

_____

_____

_____

_____

_____

I am grateful for...

Monday
_____

_____

_____

Tuesday
_____

_____

_____

Wednesday
_____

_____

_____

Thursday
_____

_____

_____

Friday
_____

_____

_____

Saturday
_____

_____

_____

Sunday
_____

_____

_____

I am grateful for...

I am grateful
for this wish...

This week I am particularly grateful for:

_____

_____

_____

_____

_____

I am grateful for...

Monday
_____

_____

_____

Tuesday
_____

_____

_____

Wednesday
_____

_____

_____

Thursday
_____

_____

_____

Friday
_____

_____

_____

Saturday
_____

_____

_____

Sunday
_____

_____

_____

I am grateful for...

I am grateful for
this abundance...

This week I am particularly grateful for:

_____

_____

_____

_____

_____

I am grateful for...

Monday
_____

_____

_____

Tuesday
_____

_____

_____

Wednesday
_____

_____

_____

Thursday
_____

_____

_____

Friday
_____

_____

_____

Saturday
_____

_____

_____

Sunday
_____

_____

_____

I am grateful for...

I am grateful
for this boldness...

This week I am particularly grateful for:

_____

_____

_____

_____

_____

I am grateful for...

Monday

_____

_____

_____

Tuesday

_____

_____

_____

Wednesday

_____

_____

_____

Thursday

_____

_____

_____

Friday

_____

_____

_____

Saturday

_____

_____

_____

Sunday

_____

_____

_____

I am grateful for...

I am grateful for
this end...

This week I am particularly grateful for:

_____

_____

_____

_____

_____

I am grateful for...

Monday
_____

_____

_____

Tuesday
_____

_____

_____

Wednesday
_____

_____

_____

Thursday
_____

_____

_____

Friday
_____

_____

_____

Saturday
_____

_____

_____

Sunday
_____

_____

_____

I am grateful for...

I am grateful for
this new beginning...

This week I am particularly grateful for:

_____

_____

_____

_____

_____

I am grateful for...

Monday _____

_____

_____

Tuesday _____

_____

_____

Wednesday _____

_____

_____

Thursday _____

_____

_____

Friday _____

_____

_____

Saturday _____

_____

_____

Sunday _____

_____

_____

Made in the USA
San Bernardino, CA
30 August 2016